Kangaroozies

"Kayla, you are in for a treat! It's time for Meghan Rose's Amazing Saturday Morning Gymnastics Show," I yelled.

Thump-thump! "Round-off!" *Thump-thump!* "Cartwheel!" *Thump-THUD.* "That doesn't count."

"Meghan, stop flopping around in front of the TV. I can't see!" Kayla whined.

I put my hands on my hips and frowned at my friend Kayla.

"So? It's just ads right now."

Kayla frowned back.

"So, I like the ads."

I narrowed my eyes, then did another cartwheel. Only this time after I landed, I kept my neck bent and swung my long brown ponytail around like a helicopter. CHOP! CHOP! CHOP!

I kept whirling until I heard Kayla take a big breath to complain again. Then I launched myself at the couch.

"EEEE!" Kayla screamed, but it sounded like she laughed a little bit too.

I like Kayla. Kayla has blond hair that's usually piggy-tailed. Plus she's kangaroo bouncy, like me. Except when she watches television. Then she's just piggy-tailed and lumpish. When I watch television, at least I stay bouncy.

I giggled, leaning back into the cushions. "OK, I'll stop."

"Thank you," Kayla said.

Another music-blasting commercial came on.

By the way, isn't it funny how the television commercials always seem louder than the shows? That is unfair, I believe, because you have to keep fiddling with the volume.

Anyway, out this music blasted. I just *had* to look at the television *scream*.

"K-K-K-K-Kangaroozies! Kangaroozies, oozies, oozies! K-K-K-K-Kangaroozies! Kangaroozies, oozies, oozies!"

The words sounded simple, but let me tell you, the tune stuck in my head the way gum sticks in your hair.

The commercial showed kids leaping through the air. They bounded as high as the treetops. And smiled. Huge smiles. Smiles so big and so toothy, they might even frighten a dentist.

The camera zoomed in on the kids' feet. They wore Kangaroozies, the ultimate high-flying, gravity-defying shoezies. With shiny silver bases and brightly colored bands, they looked like something out of a Star Wars movie.

Those Kangaroozie kids practically flew!

I've always wanted to fly. The closest I've ever come is when my neighbor let me jump on his trampoline.

I love that floating, soaring feeling, but it's hard to copy. You don't feel it jumping down stairs. You only sometimes feel it jumping on the bed or the couch.

And though I've never done it, I can't imagine you'd feel it if you jumped on the bandwagon.

I grabbed Kayla's arm. She grabbed back. We looked at each other. Her blue eyes bulged like frog eyes. My blue eyes bulged like frog eyes. And I knew the same thought pounded through our brains: *I've got to own a pair of Kangaroozies!*

"K - K - K - K - K a n g a r o o z i e s ! Kangaroozies, oozies, oozies!" she shouted.

"K - K - K - K - K a n g a r o o z i e s ! Kangaroozies, oozies, oozies!" I shouted.

We jumped on the couch and sang that stick-in-your-brain song over and over. We even turned off the TV so we could hear ourselves better.

After what seemed like a hundred million jumps, my breath ran out. I had to stop. I slouched down into the couch. Kayla joined me with a sigh. I think we both wished we had Kangaroozies under our feet instead of couch pillows.

I breathed heavily. "I can't wait to own some Kangaroozies."

Kayla nodded. "Me neither."

"I'm going to ask my mom for a pair next time we go to the store."

"Me too," Kayla said.

I had an idea. "Sometimes when I'm good, Mom buys me candy after we finish grocery shopping. I'll bet she'd let me swap Kangaroozies for candy."

"Of course," Kayla agreed. "They're only $49.99."

Uh-oh. My mouth went dry. My face felt

hot. Candy doesn't cost $49.99. Unless your breath smells super stinky and you have to buy fifty boxes of minty mints.

Plus, Mom never lets me spend more than a dollar on grocery day.

Maybe getting hold of a pair of Kangaroozies would be tougher than I thought.

Pretest

Monday rolled around without a visit to the grocery store. I told Mom about the Kangaroozies, but all she said was, "They sound like fun."

When I asked if I could have a pair, she said, "Maybe." Which is her way of saying, "If you bug me about them nonstop for three months, I might eventually wear down and consider buying them—but only if I happen to find them on sale for some shockingly low price. Otherwise, forget about them."

Still, I didn't forget about them.

I jumped up each step of the school bus that morning and BOUNCE, BOUNCE, BOUNCED down the aisle. I plopped down next to my friend Ryan, admiring his bouncy brown hair. Wish I had Kangaroozie hair like him!

"K-K-K-K-Kangaroozies, Kangaroozies, oozies, oozies," I sang over and over.

Ryan plugged his ears. "Stop it."

I slouched. "Sorry. That song keeps leaking out of my mouth."

A few minutes later, I started humming the song.

"Stop it! You're doing it on purpose just to annoy me," Ryan complained.

"Am not!" I snapped back. "I didn't even realize the song came back to my mouth!"

Then the whole thing started over again. It seems that whenever I relaxed, that zingy music came back like a bad case of poison ivy. I think it must have been contagious too, because when we finally got off the bus and hung up our backpacks, I heard Ryan singing it to himself.

I counted the steps it took for me to get to my desk.

"Thirty-three steps," I said to Kayla. "It took me thirty-three steps to get to my desk. I bet I could make it in two big bounces with Kangaroozies on."

Kayla grinned at me from her seat. "We could find out. Guess what I got yesterday?"

I felt my heart go *bump-bump*. "Kangaroozies?!"

"Yep!"

My heart sped up. *Bump-bump. Bump-bump.* "Are they shiny?"

"Super shiny."

"Are they fun?"

"Super fun."

"Do you jump high?"

"Super high."

I clapped and gasped. "Can I try them?"

Kayla shrugged. "Maybe." Which is her way of saying, "Maybe."

I almost exploded on the spot just thinking about it. Instead, the bell rang. Announcements. Calendar time. Seatwork. Soon my wiggles melted away in the same-old, same-old morning routine.

Part of that routine includes a pretest in spelling. In first grade, you take a spelling pretest every Monday.

I believe the president made that law.

11

If you get all the words right on the pretest, you don't have to take the real test on Friday. If you miss anything, the pretest shows you what words to practice that week. You do extra worksheets and homework to help you learn them.

I believe my teacher, Mrs. Arnold, made that law. Because she sure enjoys handing out those extra worksheets.

At the very beginning of the year, the spelling lists were easy. If you could spell *cat* (I could), you could spell the rest of the words on the list *(rat, fat, sat, mat, bat, hat,* and the bonus word *that)*.

I aced those pretests.

Now, just a couple months later, Mrs. Arnold gives us trickier spelling words. Hardly anyone but Lynette aces the pretests now.

I am not surprised Mrs. Arnold does this. Because if everyone gets all the words correct, she doesn't get to use her red grading pens as much. And I know she likes using her red grading pens. Plus otherwise, what would we do every Friday during spelling time?

Anyway, this week's list had *ewww* sounds, like the sound you make when someone squishes a spider or the lunch lady serves you something green and slimy. The words were *do, to, zoo, blue, few, new,* and the bonus word *threw*.

But with that Kangaroozie song buzzing around my head, I didn't really pay attention. I wrote *doozie, toozie, zoozie, bloozie, foozie, noozie,* and the bonus word *Kangaroozie*.

When I got my pretest back at the end of the day, I decided to get Mrs. Arnold a new red pen. I think she used up all the ink grading my pretest.

Mom picked me up after school. I couldn't wait to ask her if I could go to Kayla's house. She said no, we had errands to run.

I pressed my face against the car window feeling glum as a plum. A shriveled-up plum. "Where are we going?" I asked.

"Shopping," Mom said. "Your cousin David has a birthday coming up."

The only word I heard was *shopping*. I sat right straight up again, feeling not so shriveled anymore. My first chance at finding a pair of Kangaroozies lay just around the corner!

Birthday Shopping

I spotted the Kangaroozie display all the way across the store.

It looked ZINGY, ZANGY, ZIPPY.

It had a giant-size poster cutout of a jumping boy. His giant-size cardboard body made his giant-size cardboard smile even toothier. A small fan blew curly strips that were hanging down from the ceiling. They twisted like dancing noodles over the jumping boy. Shiny boxes of Kangaroozies lined the shelf behind, making the whole display sparkle the way snow does on a sunny day.

Next to the Kangaroozies, the store had wedged plain-colored playground balls, dull dart-gun games, cheap plastic jump ropes, and yawn-yawn yo-yos. Compared to them, the Kangaroozies stood out like spicy cheesy curly fries on a plate of boring baked potatoes.

Mom scanned the aisle. "How about a board game?"

I grabbed one. "Sure. This one works. Now can we look over there?" I pointed to the Kangaroozie display.

Wrinkling her nose, Mom took the game. "Pretty Posy Princess Party? For David?"

"Picky, picky." I threw it back on the shelf and grabbed another. "This one?"

"Silly Stinkbug's Sewer Monopoly." Mom handed it back. "I don't even want to *know* the property names."

Before she could object, I pulled Mom across the store toward the Kangaroozies.

"Maybe we should look around," I said.

I didn't quite make it there. Mom stopped by the dull dart-gun games. I inched over and very slowly picked a Kangaroozie box off the stack.

Mom said, "Do you think David would like the blue dart-gun game or the red one?"

I hugged the Kangaroozie box close (which was hard to do, since it was about the size of a microwave oven). "Red. And now that that's taken care of, how about buying some Kangaroozies for me?" I batted my eyelashes at her.

Mom said, "Not today, Meghan."

"Please, please, *please*, Mom?" I begged. "I almost aced my pretest in spelling today! I deserve a prize!"

Mom paused. "*Almost* aced?"

"I almost spelled most of the words almost correctly."

"How many did you get right?"

"Well, none actually. But they all started with the right letter. Almost. So can I get the Kangaroozies?"

Sighing, Mom shook her head. "Not now. Not even if you truly did ace the test. We're here to get a present for your cousin, not for you, Meghan Rose Thompson."

Excitement leaked out of me like air from a balloon with a hole. I knew there'd be no arguing. She had used my whole name.

Shoulders slumped, I slipped the box

back onto the shelf. "OK," I mumbled.

"Maybe we can buy you a pair for Christmas."

Frowning, I started counting in my head. Then stopped. (Math is not one of my better skills.) "That's more than fifty days away!"

Mom shrugged. "They'll still be here. Don't get ants in your pants."

Now, I thought about that for a minute. What did she mean by "ants in your pants"?

I've had an ant on my arm before. I didn't like it. It made my skin tickle.

I remember shaking my arm to stop the tickle.

It didn't help. I shook harder.

Then I saw that black ant. Crawling! On *me*!

Let me tell you, I slapped my arms,

SHRRRIEEKED, hopped around, and slapped my arms, SHRRRIEEKED, and hopped around again!

And that ant had only touched my arm. Imagine how I would look if a bunch of those bugs got in my pants!

I tugged Mom's sleeve. "When you say 'Don't get ants in your pants,' does it mean I shouldn't go crazy shaking some really gross bugs out of my underwear?"

Mom laughed and headed for the checkout. "No, silly. It means don't be impatient. You can't have everything right now. You can wait."

Oh. Wait.

Dragging my feet, I trailed after her.

It seems like adults are always telling you to wait. Wait until after dinner to eat that yummy-scrummy cupcake. Wait until they're done with a phone call to play your music loud. Wait until the soda stops fizzing to the top before opening the pop can all the way. Wait until your dad gets home.

Wait, wait, wait!

Don't adults understand how hard it is for us normal kid-type people to wait for something we really want? And I REALLY wanted Kangaroozies. The moment Kayla and I saw them on television, I wanted them.

And now that I had actually *touched* the Kangaroozie box with my *own* hands, I just *knew* I couldn't go on without owning a pair.

Still, I left the store empty-handed.

Oh, except for that dull dart-gun game for David.

When we got into the car, I had

disappointment marked all over my face like Mrs. Arnold's red pen marks all over my spelling pretest.

Mom gave me a little smile. "Be patient, Meghan Rose," she said, buckling her seat belt.

As we drove off, I crossed my arms, looked away, and didn't say anything. I scowled so much, I think my eyebrows grew together.

It seems I do, in fact, have ants in my pants.

Because I can't wait to stop waiting.

Up and Away

At recess Tuesday, Kayla, Lynette, and I jumped rope. Kayla made it through "Cherry, cherry, ding-dong" three times.

I clapped for her. "Wow, Kayla. A new record!"

Kayla bowed. "All thanks to my Kangaroozies. Jumping with them at home has made me extra bouncy all the time!"

Those words made the happy suddenly slide right off my face.

Kayla bit her lip. "Aren't you getting a pair?"

"Maybe," I said. And I meant my mom's kind of maybe.

Lynette said, "I've seen the ads. They look like giant, shiny boxes you strap on over your shoes."

Nodding, Kayla said, "Giant rubber bands crisscross over the giant boxes. You strap your feet to the middle. They remind me of mini-trampolines."

"What kind of straps?" I asked.

"Velcro, like my doll's belt, only thicker."

Lynette said, "Sounds simple enough to make if you had the straps."

"And giant rubber bands," Kayla added.

"And giant, shiny boxes," I said.

We stood very quiet after that, thinking.

From the corner of my eye, I spotted Ryan on the blacktop, bouncing rubber playground balls. His hair bounced too. Even his dangling shoelaces bounced along like hiccuping snakes.

An idea popped *BLAM* into my head.

I unbuckled my belt and pulled it loose. "You could also make Kangaroozies with something rubberishly springy and—" I gave my belt a SNAP "—a few superstrong straps."

"Get Ryan," I told Kayla. "Lynette, let me borrow your belt."

Lynette frowned as Kayla took off. "*Rubberishly* isn't a word. Besides, I think I know what you're going to do, and it won't work."

I frowned back. "So what am I going to do?"

She leaned forward. "Strap Ryan's playground balls to your feet with belts and then jump."

"That's right. The balls will be my mini-trampolines."

"It won't work. You don't have giant boxes for your feet. Without boxes around the balls, how will you keep your balance?"

I tapped my chin. "Good point. I wonder . . . what square thing could I substitute for boxes?"

I gazed at Lynette and smiled very sweetly. Her face went as pink as her fancy hair bow.

"I am NOT a square thing."

"You're not a box either," I said. "I do not hold that against you. But you can help me keep my balance."

With a sigh, Lynette nodded and took off

her belt. "OK. Just don't pull my arm off."

"Of course not," I said, reaching for her belt. "That would be impolite, I believe."

Kayla and Ryan dashed up. I explained my plan to make my own Kangaroozies.

Ryan groaned. "Please don't sing that song again."

"I promise I won't if you help out," I said, hoping my mouth would cooperate.

We slipped the belts under the balls. Next I put one hand on Kayla's shoulder and one hand on Lynette's shoulder and stepped onto the balls. I wobbled, which made Kayla squeal and Lynette gasp. But they grabbed me and held on.

When I started swaying again, Lynette said, "Hurry up, Ryan."

Ryan struggled with a belt. "There aren't enough holes to pull it tight."

Bending left and right, I snapped, "Then tie it!"

A few slip-slap seconds later, Ryan said, "Got it."

Aha! I bent my knees and then sprang up into the air, ready to fly.

The belts flopped open. The balls rolled.

And I flew *SMACK* into Ryan. Knocked one of his shoes right off. We both landed in a heap.

Ryan pushed me away. "Ow! Get off!"

"Sorry," I said.

Picking up Ryan's shoe, Lynette choked

back a giggle. The laces still dangled. "Ryan, I know you did your best, but you have never been very good at tying."

Ryan grabbed his shoe. "You try tying it then."

From the ground I gave Lynette a hopeful look. Kayla raised both her eyebrows at her because raising one eyebrow is too hard. Ryan grunted.

Finally Lynette shrugged. "OK."

So we tried it again. I stood on top of the balls. Kayla and Ryan held me up. Lynette tied the belts on.

Lynette stepped far away. She gave me the thumbs-up.

I coiled up like a curl in Ryan's hair.

Then I shot into the air. *ZOOM!*

The bounce sent me up and away.

But not up, up, and away. Because this

time the balls stayed put, but Kayla and Ryan didn't. The force of my leap made them fall over.

Landing without their support made *me* fall over. I landed SMACK at Lynette's feet.

Kayla, Ryan, and I lay sprawled on the ground like broken tree branches after a storm.

With a smirk, Lynette bent over, pulled her belt free, brushed off the dirt, and threaded her belt through her belt loops. "I told you it wouldn't work," she said, as the recess whistle blew.

Sometimes that girl is like raw spinach. Full of good stuff, but not on my list of favorites.

Another Pretest

By Wednesday, all that Kangaroozie waiting had made me extra antsy. The ad's song kept going through my head. Kayla kept talking about *her* Kangaroozies. And I still had a scrape on my knee from my failed attempt to make my own pair at recess yesterday.

Even practicing the *ewww* sound spelling words reminded me of you-know-what.

I almost cheered when Mrs. Arnold popped another pretest on us. I hoped it would distract me from thinking about . . .

"Hey, what is this?" I asked, when I looked at the sheet Mrs. Arnold handed out.

Mrs. Arnold moved next to me and put a hand on my shoulder. She does that every once in a while. Like when I raise my hand and she doesn't call on me, and I start bouncing in my seat like a monkey, going, "Ooh, ooh, ooh!"

"It's a pretest for our next math unit on measurement. It's your chance to show how much you already know about it."

"I know a lot about inches and stuff like that," Lynette bragged. "I'm good at measurement."

Mrs. Arnold raised one finger. That quieted Lynette. (I've got to learn that trick sometime.)

"I'm sure you'll do well, Lynette, but you

still have to take the pretest," Mrs. Arnold said. "Class, write your name at the top of your paper. I'll read through each question, and you write down your best answer. If you don't know, leave it blank."

Lynette raised her hand. "What if we get them all right?"

Mrs. Arnold smiled. "Then I will send you down to the computer lab each day during this math unit and let you play the Math Magician game."

My jaw dropped.

Everyone loves the Math Magician game. First a number sentence like 2 + 2 flashes on the screen. Then number answers shoot out of a hat. You control a rabbit that zaps the numbers with a wand. If you zap the right answer, the number explodes like a bomb. *BOOM!*

If you get ten problems right, the rabbit does a crazy, almost ants-in-your-pants dance.

And if the teacher isn't looking, you can dance along.

Just like that, I wanted to do my best on this pretest.

"Number one," Mrs. Arnold said. "Look at this clock. Where's the clock face?"

Easy, I thought. I wrote, "The clock faces forward. Or else you only see the back of the clock, and that is not very interesting."

"Which is bigger, twelve inches or one foot?"

I know how big twelve inches is, because I have a ruler. A ruler has twelve inches on it. It makes a nice sword when you play pirates with your friends.

I looked at my foot. Not sword material.

I wrote, "My one foot is smaller than twelve inches."

Mrs. Arnold kept going. "How many feet are in a yard—three, six, or twelve?"

Hmmm, I thought. *That depends on whose yard you're in. Nobody will set foot in Mrs. Smith's yard. But with Mom and Dad and me in my yard, we have six feet altogether.*

I wrote, "Six."

"Let's say you used a ruler and measured two words. One word was one inch long and the other word was one centimeter long. Which word is longer, the centimeter or the inch word?"

"They are both bugs," I wrote, "but a centimeter has a lot more legs."

"Finally," Mrs. Arnold continued, "read the scales. Tell how much each object in the picture weighs."

This problem stumped me. I raised my hand. "But Mrs. Arnold, there aren't any fish on my paper."

Mrs. Arnold opened and closed and opened and closed her mouth. Just like a fish (without scales) out of water.

Finally she said, "Don't worry about it, Meghan Rose," and collected my paper.

"Mrs. Arnold," I asked, "why do we take pretests anyway?"

"Pretests help prepare you for the real tests by showing me—and you—what you need to work on." Glancing at my paper, Mrs. Arnold shook her head and walked away.

I think I heard her mumble something about needing a new set of red pens.

I mumbled something about needing a new pair of Kangaroozies so I could bounce my antsy-pantsy way out of the classroom.

Feeling Stilted

On Thursday, Mom and Aunt Stephanie had made a balloon-blowing, cake-cooking, den-decorating date to prepare for David's party. So I got off at Ryan's bus stop after school. Ryan's mom fed us something green and healthy (but not spinach) and sent us into the backyard to play.

I didn't feel like shooting baskets, climbing trees, or digging in the sandbox. A screaming contest would have been nice.

Except last time Ryan and I played that, his mom got mad at us for scaring the cat.

"The poor thing shot across the room like a hairy bullet and raced up the back of my shirt," she had scolded.

So no screaming contests either. Which is a shame, because I am an excellent screamer.

I plopped down on the deck. Ryan plopped down next to me.

It was so quiet I bet you could hear a red pen drop.

Finally, Ryan said, "Want to chew gum?"

I shook my head. "Chew rhymes with kangaroo. And kangaroo reminds me of Kan—"

"I know, I know, I know!" Ryan shouted, waving his hands at me like he was afraid if I said the word *Kangaroozies* I'd sing that stick-in-your-brain song again. "How about reading some comics?"

I shook my head again. "Comics rhymes with vomics. And vomics remind me of Kanga—"

"Stop it!" Ryan interrupted. "I know something we can do. Come on."

Ryan pulled me to my feet. He dragged me into his family's tool shed. Dropping my arm, he started going through a bag of recycling materials.

"See if you can find some yarn and scissors. Look in one of those boxes." Ryan pointed to the side of the room.

Curious, I opened the nearest box and sifted through it. After all, who keeps yarn and scissors in a tool shed?

In the first box, I found nails, sandpaper,

screwdrivers, and purple Ping-Pong balls. Another big box had a garden hose curled up in the bottom, like toothpaste squeezed out of a tube. A third tiny box had cotton, felt, a glue gun, fuzzy dice, and—what do you know?—yarn and scissors.

I grabbed them. "OK!"

Ryan scooped up four large coffee cans. "Good. Wait on the deck. I'll be right back."

He ran into the house with the four coffee cans.

Minutes later, he ran back out of the house with the four coffee cans. He handed me two of them. "Mom punched holes at the top of each can."

I held one up. "The holes are on the bottom."

"Well, yes, if they had coffee in them.

But we are reusing these cans so that the unopened end is on top. Which means the holes are at the tops of the cans," Ryan said.

He tore the labels off his cans. "It looks better if you take the coffee labels off."

Next, Ryan pulled out a piece of yarn as long as his leg, doubled it, and cut it. He did that three more times and handed me two pieces of yarn.

"Thread the yarn through the top holes and tie it up here so you have a big yarn handle," he said.

I did it. "It looks like a giant, ugly, tin-can necklace."

Ryan grinned. "Now try this."

He put the cans open-side down on the ground. He held on to both yarn handles, stepped on top of his cans, and stood straight up. He was so tall, I could see up his nose.

He stepped forward, pulling up with the yarn and landing his foot with a *CLUMP*. He stepped again and again. *CLUMP*. *CLUMP*.

I clapped and squealed. "Homemade STILTS! You are a genius!"

Nodding, Ryan *CLUMP-CLUMP-CLUMPED* across the deck. "Who needs K-K-Kangaroozies, Kangaroozies, oozies, oozies?" he sang.

I stepped onto my coffee cans and *CLUMP-CLUMPED* after Ryan. As we *CLUMPED* around the deck singing that silly song, I felt a whole lot better.

Part of me thought, *If I hadn't been waiting for Kangaroozies, I never would have made these cool stilts.*

The other part of me stomped too close

to the cat. *CLUMP*. The cat leaped five feet into the air, took off with a *RRR-AWWRRR*, and latched on to the screen door.

Ryan's mom was not happy. Neither was the cat.

The cat also lost a bunch of hair. Enough to make a furry wig.

Plus, she hissed when we pried her claws out of the screen.

So much for stilts. And back to waiting for Kangaroozies.

That Prayer Thing

After Ryan's mom took the cat inside, I said, "Can we sit on the front porch until my mom comes?"

"Sure," Ryan said.

Good friends do that. Sit with you when you're feeling embarrassed and sad. Or when you've stepped on their cat.

"Sorry my mom took the stilts away," Ryan said. He sounded sorry too.

"I will live. The cat will live too."

Ryan nodded. "We should have made stilts for the cat," he joked.

"Very funny," I grumbled.

Then I pounded my fist in my hand. "Why can't my mom just buy me a pair of Kangaroozies? This whole mess wouldn't have happened."

Ryan slapped his forehead. "Oh, right! Then instead of stepping on the cat with stilts you could have squished it with Kangaroozies. Much better."

I glared at him. "You're mean!"

"Well, it's true!" he shouted back.

Since he was probably right, I just crossed my arms and harrumphed at him.

For a moment, Ryan fiddled with his untied shoelace. Finally, he puffed up his cheeks, then blew out the air. "Did you try that prayer thing?"

He caught me by surprise. "What?"

Ryan kept his eyes down and talked in a soft voice. "That prayer thing. Last time, at the talent show, you had a problem and you prayed about it. I remember how praying helped you figure out what to do. I pray now too when I've got a problem. And guess what? Praying helps."

He let his shoelace flop on the ground. "Well, mostly. I pray at dinner too, but it doesn't help. Because that's a thank-you kind of prayer and not a please-help-me kind of prayer. Unless Dad's cooking, and then it's both."

Now, I *know* prayer helps. And I felt bad I didn't think of it myself. Maybe because Ryan did think of it and I didn't, my stomach hardened up like play clay left out in the sun.

I clenched my teeth. "I can solve this problem on my own. I don't need to pray."

"But you couldn't make your own pair of Kangaroozies," Ryan pointed out. "And the stilts didn't work out either."

"I know," I said, very grumpy. "Which means Mom has to buy them for me."

"Or you'll have to buy your own. And that's a lot of spare change."

I hung my head. "I know."

A cat hair tickled my chin. I pulled it off my collar and let it fall from my fingertips. It floated down and stuck to my pants.

"Sorry about your cat," I said. I pulled the hair off again and watched it fall.

"It's OK," Ryan said. "Hair grows back."

Grinning a little, I said, "Yours did after I cut it."

"That's right!" Ryan touched his head, as if he were checking.

I snipped at Ryan's hair with my fingers, but he ducked and laughed. "That was the shortest haircut I've ever had. You could make a ton of money cutting hair for the army! They always wear short, short, short haircuts."

I said, "Too bad there's not an army around here."

"Yeah," Ryan said. "Too bad."

An idea popped *BLAM* into my head. There may not be an army around here, but there were a lot of boys around here.

I glanced sideways at Ryan. "Could you call your friends and ask them to bring money to school tomorrow? I'm setting up shop at recess."

Ryan frowned. "I think I know what

you're going to do, and it won't work."

I frowned back. "You sound like Lynette. So what am I going to do?"

"Charge money to give people short army haircuts. But Mrs. Arnold will never let you bring scissors on the playground, so it won't work."

I hadn't thought of that. "Hmmm. I'll sell something," I said.

Ryan cocked his head. "What?"

"Something. Just trust me and spread the word, OK?"

Shrugging, Ryan said, "OK."

Good friends do that too. Give you an OK when you need it most.

Mom pulled up. She tooted the horn. I ran to the car. "See ya!"

"You could always sell cookies!" Ryan yelled after me.

Not a bad idea. I gave Ryan a thumbs-up.

"Mom," I said, as we pulled away from the curb, "do we have any Oreo cookies?"

"No."

"Can you bake some cookies?"

"Not tonight," she said.

My stomach flopped, but I thought fast. *What else could I sell?* "Got any lemonade?"

"Sorry."

"Marshmallows?"

"I can get some on my next trip to the grocery store."

I scrunched up my face. "What *do* we have?"

Mom thought. "Soup, milk, cereal, leftover casserole, and a bag of potatoes."

Not much to work with. But I will live.

I took a big breath. "Can I take the potatoes to school tomorrow?"

Kangaroozie Quarters

I do and don't like Fridays.

I like Fridays because the lunch ladies always serve pizza. Maybe they need a break and pizza is easy to make.

Or maybe they serve pizza because they are out of ketchup by Friday.

Or maybe they just plain lack imagination.

Another good thing about Fridays is that Mrs. Arnold gives us something she calls

Chatter Matters time. She says we need "occasions to interact in a positive manner with classmates."

That means talking together without arguing, tattling, or bragging.

So right before lunch, for fifteen minutes we sit in groups of two or three and whisper-talk about whatever we want. We can sit all over the room too, even under Mrs. Arnold's desk!

Still, I *don't* like Fridays because they are test days. There's always the spelling test, and often other end-of-the-unit tests too.

Like next Friday, Mrs. Arnold plans on giving us the math unit test plus the spelling test. She'll probably throw in a social studies or science test too, just because sometimes she needs to get all those tests out of her system the way I sometimes need to run around to get all the wiggles out of my system.

This week, since I missed every single spelling word on the pretest, I had to study, study, study my words every night. At least my *ewww* work paid off. I turned in a perfect doozy of a paper.

I also don't like Fridays because Mrs. Arnold often acts like her brain is somewhere else. For example, one Friday I told her a great joke about dogs not liking hammers because they don't like the pound. Instead of laughing and saying "Ha ha, nice joke, Meghan," Mrs. Arnold just sighed and said, "That's nice. Find your seat."

Another Friday I warned her I might smell during the day because I ate an entire jar of pickles for a bedtime snack. Instead of pinching her nose and saying "Phew!" she just sighed and said, "That's nice. Find your seat."

But this Friday I liked Mrs. Arnold acting like her brain was far away. Because when I dragged in a ten-pound bag of potatoes and announced that I'd be selling Spuddy Buddies at noon, she didn't take them away. She just sighed and said, "That's nice. Find your seat."

Hooray for Fridays!

When Chatter Matters started, six kids crowded Mrs. Arnold, begging for the under-the-desk spot. I tugged her arm and held up a potato.

"Mr. Spuddy Buddy wants to join my group."

Mrs. Arnold just sighed and said, "That's nice. Find your seat."

Bouncing like a kangaroo, I rushed over

to Kayla and Lynette at the reading couch and then held out my Spuddy Buddy.

In black permanent marker, I had drawn a robot on a potato. It had a square face, two knobby antennas, round eyes, and a straight line mouth.

Kayla whisper-squealed. "How cute! Can I hold it?"

As Kayla turned the spud around in her hands, Lynette leaned over her shoulder for a closer look. "What is it?"

I wiggled my eyebrows. "A Spuddy Buddy. I'm selling them at lunch for a quarter apiece. I'm trying to earn enough money to buy my own pair of Kangaroozies."

Kayla gave it a little toss. "Good idea. Are they all robots?"

"No," I said. "I only made one for a sample. People can buy a potato and draw their own special Spuddy Buddy face."

"You'll need a lot of markers then," Lynette said.

My body sagged. "Uh-oh. I only have two markers."

Kayla whisper-squealed again. "I know! I'll do all the drawing for you."

"I can help too," Lynette said quickly. "I like drawing."

I pulled the black markers out of my back pocket. Biting my lip, I paused, thinking about their offers.

Kayla made a puppy-dog face. "Please? I'll do it for free."

I gave a half smile. "Deal."

Kayla clapped. "Let's make a sign to advertise."

"*I'll* make the sign," Lynette said in a firm voice. "I can spell."

"Meghan!" a voice hissed from behind the couch. I looked over the edge. Ryan sat with Adam and Levi. He pointed at my Spuddy Buddy. "What's that?"

By the time Chatter Matters ended,

everyone was whisper-talking about Spuddy Buddies. Kids saved their milk money just so they could buy potatoes at recess. Abigail even asked if she could buy a Spuddy Buddy with big eyelashes!

After lunch, Lynette hung up her sign by the playground bars. Kids surrounded us. We drew aliens, kitties, sharks, bunnies, and dinosaurs.

Spuddy Buddies sold like hot potatoes.

When the lunch recess whistle finally blew, my pocket jingled with quarters.

Kangaroozie quarters.

No Luck

"Four-fifty, four-seventy-five, five, five-twenty-five," Lynette counted. "Good job, Meghan. You made five dollars and twenty-five cents."

My smile dropped. I stuffed my take-home folder into my backpack. Adam rolled a Spuddy Buddy past me as he lined up for the bus.

"Are you sure you counted right?" I choked out.

Lynette nodded. "Positive. I counted it twice."

In a voice much cheerier than I felt, Kayla said, "I came up with twenty-one dollars."

Lynette said, "That's because there are twenty-one quarters and you counted each as a dollar."

"So?" Kayla said.

Lynette folded her arms. "So quarters are only worth twenty-five cents each, not a dollar each. And since you need a hundred cents to make a whole dollar, Meghan made less than six dollars, *not* twenty-one."

"Never mind," I interrupted, scooping up the coins. They felt heavy in my hands. I wanted to throw them all away. Instead, I split the pile two ways.

"Thanks for helping. That's for you guys," I said.

"Yay!" Kayla said. "I like working for free!"

Lynette looked at me, and my face turned red. I'm sure she knew I had failed again and was back to wait, wait, waiting for Kangaroozies.

Dragging my feet, I walked toward the door. Lynette caught up and put her arm around me.

Kayla bounded up and knocked us over. "Let's do it again!" she said.

She also dropped her quarters. They hit the floor with a *TING-TING-TING*.

Then they rolled off like scared rabbits. If rabbits rolled, that is.

"Pick that up, please, ladies," Mrs. Arnold called from her desk.

Dropping my backpack, I knelt. Without a word, I started collecting the coins.

Giving Kayla a sharp look, Lynette helped. "It's OK, Meghan," she said. "You'll feel better later."

But I didn't feel better later. Because later I went to my cousin David's party. And guess what he got for his birthday?

Kangaroozies, of course.

My mom took a million pictures of him bouncing all over the place like a rocket.

She also took pictures of me standing next to him very unbouncily, planted in the ground like a telephone pole.

A telephone pole crawling with ants.

Ants STILL in My Pants

Still awake at 9:47 PM, I watched Mom print off the pictures at home. Each photo caused those crushing I-gotta-have-it feelings to roll over me again.

I fumed like a snorting bull before it charges. "It's not fair."

Mom turned off the printer. "What's not fair?"

"David got Kangaroozies and I didn't."

"It's not your birthday."

Impatience crashed through me like a baseball through a window. I stomped my foot. I gritted my teeth. I fisted my hands. I shouted, "I want a pair of Kangaroozies!"

Mom's lips made a long thin line. "Well, control that craving, kiddo. You'll have to wait, because it's not happening right now." She looked me in the eye. I swallowed hard. "Especially after that little outburst."

Mom sounded so firm, it took the steam out of me. I hung my head, feeling suddenly ashamed.

Mom pulled the latest photo album off the shelf, sat at the desk, and started putting pictures into place. I grabbed the nearest photo album and sank into the couch.

Ah. My baby album. Me with a rattle in my mouth. Me with the telephone in my mouth. Me with my foot in my mouth. Me with food everywhere but in my mouth.

Mom finally joined me. I wanted to kiss her and say I was sorry. Instead, I let her look over my shoulder.

"You were cute," she said.

Nodding, I pointed to a picture of me in a bouncy seat. "I still am. And look! Even then I jumped like a . . . kangaroo . . . zie."

Mom chuckled. "You just don't give up, do you?"

I shook my head.

With a tiny smile, Mom ran a finger down the edge of the picture. "Waiting is one of the hardest things to do. It's still hard for me as an adult. Believe it or not, I know how you feel wanting something really badly. So badly you can hardly think about anything else. I wanted something like that once."

"What was it?"

"I wanted a baby. I wanted you, Meghan Rose."

I sat up a little bit. What did she mean?

Mom continued. "After Dad and I married, I longed for a baby of my own to love. Aunt Stephanie had two babies. Most of my friends had babies. But I didn't."

"A year passed and then another. No baby. I worried. I prayed. I even visited a special doctor. Still no baby."

"I was tired of waiting. Almost . . ." She paused and gave me a thoughtful glance. "Almost angry."

I held my breath.

"For six years I prayed and I hoped and I waited. I begged God for a child until I thought he wasn't even listening anymore. I felt like—"

"A balloon with a hole?" I offered, letting my air out.

Mom nodded. "Only the hole was in my heart."

"And then?" I asked.

"Then you came along and filled it right up." Mom pulled me into a hug, and I leaned into her.

"God taught me something," Mom whispered, her arm still holding me close. "He always listens. And when he tells us to wait, he'll wait right there with us, calming our worries and holding our hands."

I thought about that for a minute. "So if I have ants in my pants, does that mean God has let go of my hand?"

Laughing, Mom shook her head. "No. It more likely means you've let go of his."

Wow. Well, maybe I did feel extra antsy

because I had let go of God's hand. But Mom's waiting seemed different from mine. Maybe even easier. After all, you don't have a choice about waiting with a baby.

Unlike Kangaroozies, babies don't sit right there in the store ready to go. It's a good thing too. How would you keep babies from pulling the price tags off their foreheads?

Also unlike Kangaroozies, babies would spoil like milk if you left them on the shelf too long, I'm sure. Mom wonders all the time if I'm spoiled. But I doubt that could ever happen to me. I would never sit on a shelf long enough to spoil.

Then again, even though you don't find babies on a shelf in the store, there are an awful lot of them around. It might be hard watching people enjoy their babies when you couldn't have one.

Heart-achy hard.

Hard like watching David with his Kangaroozies.

I yawned.

"Oh my!" Mom said. "It's late. Off to bed, you."

I Get It Now

After Mom tucked me into bed, I finally decided to pray about my problem.

"Hello, God. I've got a bug problem. Ants. And let me tell you, they're in my pants! I think you could get rid of those ants if you sent me a pair of Kangaroozies. Please? Amen."

When I finished, I lay in bed with my eyes wide open, feeling a little bit comforted but still kind of uncomfortable.

I felt comforted because when I prayed, I knew God listened.

But I felt uncomfortable too. Because even though part of me hoped to find a pair of Kangaroozies under my pillow in the morning like when the tooth fairy leaves a quarter . . . another part of me knew God didn't work that way.

I stared at the darkness around me. I wondered why I felt so impatient.

I wondered why I didn't pray about it sooner.

And I wondered if God would have waited even longer for me to come to talk to him about Kangaroozies.

And then I realized, he would. He would wait. Because he loves me that much.

You know, I'm glad God is a good waiter.

I don't mean a waiter like the one who brings the food you order at a restaurant.

I mean a waiter like when you wait for the waiter to bring the food *after* you order.

God would never get tired of waiting at the table. He'd wait and wait and smile and wait.

Not me. I'd chew my napkin, flip spoons, complain, and spill my drink.

One question still bothered me. Unable to sleep, I talked to God again.

"Hello, God, I'm back. Listen, I understand making someone wait a long time for something important like a baby, although that still bothers me a little. But why should we wait to buy things our parents can get right away? Why wait for anything?"

Do you ever feel like God's telling you

something but you don't actually hear his voice? That's kind of how I felt just then.

In the quiet of my room, with the night-light glowing softly, a strange subject came to me—the pretests I took that week in spelling and math.

Mrs. Arnold had said, *"Pretests help prepare you for the real tests by showing me—and you—what you need to work on."*

I let that thought roll around in my mind for a while until it snagged on something. Then an idea popped *BLAM* into my head.

Suppose this waiting thing worked like a pretest. If so, what did it show me I needed to work on?

One word came to mind. *Patience*. And *self-control*.

OK, maybe two words.

Anyway, I bet waiting helps you learn

patience. And patience helps you control yourself.

Self-control would have been handy when I got hold of shaving cream in school last month. I didn't wait for directions from Mrs. Arnold before shaking up two cans and spraying foam all over the reading table. Being able to control that craving for shaving would have saved me a whole lot of cleaning up time, I believe.

Also, self-control would be handy when I have to wait in line at the drinking fountain. If I could self-control my arms, I wouldn't get in trouble for pushing so much.

Maybe waiting isn't such a bad thing. Just a hard thing, like Mom said.

And sometimes hard things teach us skills we need to learn.

"I get it now, God," I whispered. "Maybe

waiting will teach me patience. And self-control. Then maybe I can self-control the ants in my pants. After all, I know I *can* wait. I've waited one week already."

I gave myself a little pat on the back.

"Guess what else? While I waited, I invented something. I learned how to make stilts. And I started a potato business. And that's not a bad deal."

My eyelids grew heavy. "Thanks for listening, God," I added. "Sorry I didn't ask you about this stuff sooner."

Warm under my covers, I drifted off to sleep.

I dreamed about flying . . . without Kangaroozies.

At least . . . not yet.

Chatter Matters

1. Describe a time when you wanted something. What was it? Why did you want it? Did you get it? If not, how did you feel? What did you try to do to get it? If you did get it, how long did you enjoy it?

2. How do commercials and ads on TV and in magazines affect how much you want something? Does it matter to you what kinds of toys, clothes, or games your friends have? Why or why not?

3. Why do you think waiting is hard? How do you pass the time waiting in the doctor's office? on a car ride? How do you act when you are waiting in a line for a drink at the water fountain? a movie? a roller coaster?

4. What do you think the Bible says about waiting? Find out by looking up Psalm 27:14; Psalm 40:1; Romans 8:25; Romans 12:12; and Ephesians 4:2. Which verse is your favorite? Explain to someone what that verse means to you and how you might use it to help you wait. What do you think it means to wait on God? What can help you to be more patient?

5. In some situations, you should not wait to act. In an emergency, call 911 right away. And don't wait to apologize when you do something wrong. Can you think of other situations when you should not wait?

Blam! – Great Activity Ideas

1. Make stilts. You will need two large, empty tin cans (coffee cans work well) and string. Ask an adult to punch two holes into each can opposite each other, one on each side of the can. The holes should be close to the rim of the can on the unopened end. (If the open end of the tin can has a sharp edge, ask an adult to cover it with duct tape.)

Then cut two pieces of string, each twice as long as your leg. Thread one string through the holes in a can and tie the string ends together. Do the same with the other string. Stand up on the cans, pull the strings tight, and walk. Note: Two soup cans duct-taped together can be substituted for one coffee can. Instead of making holes, slip the string under the duct tape between the two cans.

2. Make a parachute! Meghan Rose invented her own Kangaroozies, using playground balls and belts. You can invent something too—a parachute! Gather a plastic shopping bag, string, tape, a paper cup, cotton, a zipper-sealed plastic sandwich bag, and an egg. With these materials, and with help from a friend or a parent, design a parachute that will carry the egg safely to the ground. Ask an adult to launch the parachute outside.

Will your egg survive the fall? Or will it crack? Note: Before launching, place the egg in the zipper-sealed plastic sandwich bag to help prevent messes!

3. Make a Spuddy Buddy. You will need a potato and a black permanent marker. Simply draw on the potato. If you feel extra creative, use felt, cotton, or paper to make a hat or other clothes for your spud. Use toothpicks or glue to attach these extra bits.

4. Test time. How good are you at spelling? Rearrange the letters from the phrase *I've got ants in my pants!* and see how many words you can make. Some examples: *any, vet, ten*.

Scoring: 0–5 words = Not bad. (I already gave you three!!) 6–8 words = You spell well. 9–11 words = You are a stellar speller! 12 or more words=When it comes to spelling, you're a word WIZARD!

5. Make a sand timer. You will need two small, clear plastic cups of the same size, sand, an empty cereal box or other piece of thin cardboard, a pencil, a hole punch, scissors, and tacky glue. First, place a cup upside down on the cardboard and trace around the mouth of the cup to make a circle. Cut the circle out. Stay just outside the line as you cut. Use the hole punch to make five or six holes in the cutout.

Fill about ¼ of one cup with sand. Next, put glue carefully around the rim of that cup. Center the cutout circle on top of the glue. Make sure your cutout covers the mouth of the cup completely so no sand can escape out the sides.

Then put a line of glue on the rim of the

other cup and place that cup upside down (open end down) on top of the cutout circle. Allow to dry. Once dry, flip the cups over and watch the sand fall from the top cup to the bottom one. Count how many seconds or minutes it takes for all the sand to fall into the bottom cup.

For my parents—LZS

For Mandy—SC

Lori Scott, a graduate of Wheaton College and former first grade teacher, loves creative science and math activities, drama and art, the Sunday comics, and . . . red pens!

Lori has published numerous devotions, short stories, poems, articles, and puzzles for children, teens, and adults. Although she created the Meghan Rose series for her daughter, Meghan, her son, Michael, enjoys reading the books too.

Look for more Meghan Rose secrets and surprises coming online soon!

Stacy Curtis is a cartoonist, illustrator, and printmaker whose illustrations have appeared in several magazines, newspapers, and children's books.

Stacy grew up in Kentucky and graduated with a degree in graphic design from Western Kentucky University. He and his wife, Jann, now live in Oak Lawn, Illinois and happily share their home with their dog, Derby. Stacy's artwork can be found on the Web at www.stacycurtis.com.